FROM IDEA TO MONEY

Practical Insights To Help You Win Big With Your Ideas

SECOND EDITION

BRIAN REUBEN

FROM IDEA TO MONEY

Practical Insights To Help You Win Big With Your Ideas

SECOND EDITION

BRIAN REUBEN

Except where otherwise stated, all scriptures are taken with permission from the King James translation of the Holy Bible.

ISBN-13:978-1535402484

ISBN-10:1535402482

Printed in the United States of America.

I dedicate this book to my lovely kids, Sunesis and Darryl.

CONTENTS

ACKNOWLEDGMENTS

I acknowledge Dr. Ikechi Ogbonnaya, Engr. Emmanuel Iroham, Mr. Tochukwu Uche and my lovely wife Charisa for their amazing support and dedication our ministry.

THE HIDDEN SECRET OF THE MASTERS

(Author's Amazing Preface)

Why did executives sit on the bare floor to hear Bill Gates make a speech in 1992 in Atlanta?

If you have the right answer, then you know the secret to turning any idea to money. I've had the privilege of meeting and sharing thoughts with some of the most respected and idolized personalities that have walked this earth. I have spoken to the brightest of minds in business, politics, and just about any field you can think of.

I have listened to Kings. I have heard Presidents of Nations; I have shared moments with some of the greatest Army Generals dead and alive. In the course of my life I have made friends with some of the most powerful religious leaders. I mean men and women who have shook this world, whose choices have become laws, the brightest, I mean the brightest in just about any field you can think of.

At the same time, I have know some worst of failures. Men and women who failed at just anything you can think of. I have also heard them. They have shared their thoughts with me. I have looked into their minds and seen why they failed.

Brace Up, This Can Change Your Life

In your opinion why do you think some people win while others loose? Why are some people absolutely successful while others struggle through life?

Successful people agree: Wining in life is not about the work you are involved in. It has nothing to do with certificate. It is not about your place of birth. It's not about your race or nationality or even you whether born poor or rich. For example

The Dejected Youngman

In 1923, the world advertising genius, Bruce Barton told a story of a confused and dejected young man who visited him. The man was a sales manager with a reputation of writing sale letters. But suddenly this was man out of work and depressed, even suicidal.

Barton led the man to a window and began:

Look out there at those buildings" Barton said. "All filled with offices. Business offices. Offices of people who have goods to sell and most of whom don't know how to sell them" You say you can write sales letters. This is your great chance to prove it. Write those people a letter that will sell them the idea that they need you to help them sell their goods. The man accepted challenge. Six month later his earning were over $25,000 a year - that's in 1923. How did he achieve that?

"This Is Your Victory."

If there is anyone out there who still doubts that America is a place where all things are possible; who still wonders if the dream of our founders is alive in our time; who still questions the power of our democracy, tonight is your answer.

With those words the son of a Black man from Kenya, Barak Obama took the stage and stood as the very expression of the idea that The United States of America has transcended the ultimate race barrier even at a time it seemed absolutely impossible breaking the stronghold of many years. How was that possible?

They Defiled The Winter

On a cold winter night in January 1936, two thousand five hundred men and women flooded into the grand ballroom of Hotel Pennsylvania in New York. Every available seat was filled by half past seven. At eight o'clock, the eager crowd was still pouring in. The spacious balcony was soon congested.

Even getting a space to stand was a premium and hundreds of people, tired after a stressful day in business, stood up for an hour and half to witness one of the most life transforming moments ever!

They were eager to get important information that will see them through the upward spiral in life and business. The secret that has driven men and women to the top. Every great man or woman who ever lived knew it. But what's this secret?

Imagine... Executives Sat Cross-Legged On The Floor

In June 1992, in Atlanta, at an annual computer trade show known as *Comdex*, people lined up for two city blocks to hear someone make a speech. Executives in business suits spilled out into the aisles arid sat cross-legged on the floor when the seats were filled. What were they waiting for? To hear Bill Gates make a speech. That's all. They wanted to see what they can learn from the famous computer mermaid, they came to discover the same secret. They came to learn how to work their ideas and turn it into global brands.

The Big Question

The question is how did these people have so many people to believe in their idea thereby turning their ideas into global brands successfully and becoming exceedingly rich in essence? Have you ever seen a best selling book? What about a bottle of coke? A Nokia phone? ... That's an idea turned brand and that's the secret that made Bill Gates very rich. That's why Trump is a Billionaire. That's why Obama is the President of the United States.

But what's the secret anyway? It is the ability to talk and have people listen, agree and follow you. That's all. Whatever it is you are selling, a political idea, business idea or faith idea. Whether you want a job, close a sale, win a deal or get a contract. That's all you need to know. That's the difference between where you are and where you want to be. How to propose persuasively, that's the skill you are looking for.

No matter what your idea may be, if you do not know how to talk about it and get your intended audience listen and agree with you, you cannot make a cent out of it not to talk of becoming a success with it.

"We possess within us a marvelous force of incalculable power, which gives us mastery over ourselves and others…" Emile Coue, the 19th century French Professor was known to have said those words.

What power was he referring to and how you can use it to your utmost advantage?

Ben Franklin said, "Give me 26 lead soldiers and I will conquer the world."

What did Benjamin Franklin mean when he said that? Simply this: Franklin knew that his printing press, loaded with the 26 letters of the alphabet, packed more power than any artillery when it came to revolution. Two centuries have gone by, and yet the world hasn't quite recovered from the monumental changes Franklin brought into being with just ink and paper.

If you want to command influence, get rich and overwhelmingly successful, you MUST master the art of effective selling your ideas. Whether you are sending an application, letter for contract or even seeking romance with an attractive lady, this is the skill you need. Remember the salesman I told you about earlier? Ask yourself, exactly what did he write that made people who knew nothing about him agree to give him lots of money? Do you think it was just a stroke of luck that got Bill Gates so rich? What about Donald Trump? How did all these people become successful at least in wealth and fame? Here's the secret- they know how to persuade people to buy into their ideas.

Are you ready? Fasten your seat belt we are about to take off...

Brian Rueben.

CHAPTER 1

THE SECRET THAT TURNS IDEAS TO MONEY!

The people curse him who holds back grain [when the public needs it], but a blessing [from God and man] is upon the head of him who sells it. - Proverbs 11:26 (*Amplified*)

It's pretty safe to assume that you have an idea you are hoping to realize. Of course that's why you picked this book up. But then I want to ask you a question. Why haven't you manifested your idea yet?

If you answered anything less than an honest *I'm working it out*, then you may never turn it to money except you change your language. Money, environment, technology and nothing at all is an issue. What's keeping you is a simple information. Interestingly, the answer you need is here.

God made the world in the beginning, but Genesis 2:5 spoke of a *time When no plant of the field was yet in the earth and no herb of the field had yet sprung up, for the Lord God had not [yet] caused it to rain upon the earth and there was no man to till the ground,* So God needed someone to help Him and so do you. What you need then is to understand how to talk others into partnership with you. No one has birthed an idea all alone. You need to learn how to propose your ideas to the right people. That's all!

Let me be totally honest to you now. I knew nothing about e-books before I met a certain young man, back in my days as the CEO of a publishing company in Nigeria.

The gentleman walked into our office and asked to see me. Chances played on his favour that very day because I understood he has sought to see me time and time again.

He didn't look like someone I could do business with but I gave him the chance to talk.

"I saw your advert in town." He began "Okay, you'll like to publish a book with us", I responded. "Yes, but my own is an e-book "He responded. "Ebook?" I thought. "What's it all about?"

Then the guy gave me about 30 minutes lesson on digital publishing and what benefits my company stands to gain.

He just needed a little money to finish up some of the things he already started. Just N45, 000, really.

He wanted to give me the whole details. "Don't brother, do me a proposal and let me have it on my table first thing tomorrow morning." I told him.

His proposal made sense and we did business together.

The N45, 000 we gave him brought in over a million naira for us and the guy made millions of naira from his ebook business. He was happy, we were happy.

What brought about the entire thing? Someone believed in his idea enough to talk to another about it.

The bank sponsored it

I thought of a new television program and then sent out letter proposals to some companies in my city. I needed them to sponsor my new television program and ran advert on the program.

A few weeks later responses came in a bank contacted me to have their advert on the program for a whole year.

They asked for sponsorship. The cost I gave them took care of the program for six months.

Again, what was the secret? I got them to partner with us!

It worked on MTN too!

At a certain association where I was the president, we planned to organize a dinner where we also hoped to raise money. But, I didn't want us to spend our money on the program. I just knew we could have a better way.

Why? I know how the world works. I told our secretary to propose the sponsorship to one of the biggest companies in Africa.

A few weeks later, I got a call on my cell phone. The management of the company was contacting me asking for a convenient time to meet with me. The deal worked and MTN sponsored our event. We had more money than we needed.

Again, how did that come about? A proposal.

Money without a guarantor?

The first company I established was financed by a man I never met until I sent him a proposal. He rented the office, bought fixtures and fittings and other office equipment, provided the funds for incorporation as well as working capital for the business. We got the business rolling very fast. How could I have achieved that, a young man without business experiences? A proposal worked the magic.

You see the very reason why so many fail in business or fail to even start the business at all for the excuse of not having the needed money is simple, lack of knowledge.

Here's an important point: People are constantly seeking to solve problems whether as individuals or corporate institutions. The money you require to manifest your idea so money will start following is in someone's account right now. How do you locate this person? I'll give you the answer but you must understand this...

CHAPTER 2

WHY NATIONS EXIST.

A nation is any group of people possessing certain characters in common, by which they are distinguished from all others. By this therefore, a nation is defined beyond the idea of people living together within a geographical setting to any group of people bound by a common interest. That means as the United States, Canada, Australia and Nigeria are nations, so is the banking would bound by their interest in finance, legal world bound by their interest in the law etc.

But why do nations exist?

When in the Course of human events it becomes necessary for one people to dissolve the political bands which have connected them with another and to assume among the powers of the earth, the separate and equal station to which the Laws of Nature and of Nature's God entitle them, a decent respect to the opinions of mankind requires that they should declare the causes which impel them to the separation.

We hold these truths to be self-evident, that all men are created equal, that they are endowed by their Creator with certain unalienable Rights, that among these are Life, Liberty and the pursuit of Happiness. - **Thomas Jefferson in *the Declaration of Independence.***

Those words define why the United States exist. They wanted a society where people can live in freedom and happiness.

In Nigeria the government stated that they want a land of freedom with equal opportunities for all. That's why they exist.

The legal profession (nation) exists to ensure justice. They exist for a reason.

What do you see here? Nations exist to solve problems. The purpose of ideas is to solve problems.

Where does your idea belong? Can it help the Nigerian government build a land of freedom with equal opportunity for all? Then you'll need to talk to the Nigerian government about your idea. Can it help the banking nation provide better financial solutions? Then you must talk to the banks, you are the man they seek!

How?

Let look at it this way. Banking evolved because people need a safe place to keep their money. As they continued to exist, they kept on discovering and meeting unmet needs in the society.

Stock brokering firms exist because people have need to broker stock. Their existence afford people the chance to easily secure ownership of various companies of their choice.

Marketing companies exist because there is a need to assist people and organizations sell their products and services.

The money and the profit is not the core of their existence, it is an effect of their services. This understanding is very important. Companies exist to solve people's problem. They require ideas to solve the problems and they don't have all the ideas, for anyone that does will rule the world.

Got it?

Knowing that nations exist to solve problems, you can now be sure that they will be ready to do business with you if what you are proposing falls in line with the solution they provide.

Understand this, nations have specific vision and mission, and everything done in that nation whether it is employment, divesting, contracting or anything at all must fall in line with this vision. This means that you cannot propose effectively unless you already know the company and understand their purpose completely. As a matter of fact there will be no need no need proposing if you lack this knowledge.

Remember the Youngman l told you about who came and talked to me about contract publishing his e-book ? Now do you sincerely think l would have had anything to do with him if I do not already offer contract publishing?

Probably no. Keep this principle in mind before anything else.

Two things happen when you gain this understanding that companies are willing to accept, read your proposal and do business with you.

Firstly, it conditions your spirit and shapes your mind. It gives you the right mental construction you require to win the business you need. Know this; you cannot win any business if your mental construction is wrong.

Secondly, you go ahead and propose the business knowing that nations actually need your ideas to move forward.

If you do not know this, you will be defeated even before you start. This is the major secret of those who turn ideas to money. Settle this in your mind now.

But it does not end there. Now I know what nations are and why they exist, how do I get them hooked to my idea?

This page is intentionally left blank

CHAPTER 3

HOW TO UNCOVER A NEED

Whether you are responding to a Request For Proposal (RFP) or you are sending an unsolicited proposal, bear this in mind; needs already exist they are merely identified.

Really, every nation has a purpose which they express as vision, mission or declaration of purpose. That's what defines what they do, where they go, when they go there and how they do that. You've got to know that.

If you can know who a man is and where he wants to go to it will be a lot easier to help him get there. The vision is where they want to go to, their mission is how they want to get there If therefore you can understand these two you can easily know what a business need and hence how you can help them.

But if you lack this information you are blind about them, so you cannot help them. How can you help someone you don't know where he is going to? How would you be talking to man who wants to take a flight to Lagos to meet up with an appointment in the next one hour that your bus will get him there at most within five hours? That will be a waste effort; he will not even listen to you.

So you've got to know their vision and mission to know their need. And this is simple, most nation and businesses have websites today and there you can get any information you want about them. But even for those that do not, there are other ways to do this. Pay them a visit, ask questions, get their brochure, just get to know them.

WHAT IS A PROPOSAL?

Proposal as I consider it in this book is any expression directed at somebody or a group with the intention of getting a predetermined result.

Whether it is a stare, a company logo on the television, a flier, a smile or whatever it is so longer as it is directed from one person to another with the intention of getting a predetermined result, it is a proposal.

The predetermined result could be to get a date with an attractive lady, get a job with a company or to close a deal. It could be to convince people to buy your product, your idea, vote for you or marry you.

That's what it is. It could be written or oral. Because of what I intend to achieve which is to help you understand how to communicate to win and have your prospect love you for that I will not devote time to the structure of a proposal. I want you to become an effective communicator whether in writing or orally.

WHEN TO PROPOSE

No doubt you've been to a restaurant before. When do you think is the right time for the waiter to ask for your order? You and I know it's quite unlikely for the waiters to stand on the way looking at people, approaching them with a smile and softly asking what they would like to eat.

But, the moment you walk into the restaurant and sit down, one will necessarily come for your order. At sometimes however, you may just have to call the waiter because they might seem to be very busy and thus ignore you.

Here's the point: The world is the restaurant and people coming into the restaurant represent the companies (businesses). Once a company opens its doors for business, the company has opened its doors for proposals no matter how small they might be. They'll either invite everybody to submit proposals to know how they can work together or you figure it out yourself and go for it. But be sure of this, they want to read your proposal.

You say, but I heard companies turn unsolicited proposals into the refuse bin? True! But, who told you they do not take a look at them before turning them in? Who told you people have not done business with them through unsolicited proposals?

You say so how do I do that? Well, that's why you are reading this book.

Before we continue let us look at the two types of proposals used in the business world

SOLICITED PROPOSAL

Solicit means an request addressed to someone of superior status. when a company or somebody says "do me a proposal" it means you have crossed a level one. They have firmly asked you to show them how you can solve their problem.

The need could be to supply a product, fill vacant positions or to get business ideas.

But what I want to consider here is a case when a company solicits for proposals publicly. That is when they make a public request for proposal from anybody who can offer what they want. In this case normally they spell out what they want (may be building an office block), conditions for submitting the proposals, qualifications, who should apply and the offer closing date. In this case everybody is free to apply so long as you meet the conditions.

This book however will not dwell on this type of proposal

UNSOLICITED PROPOSALS

Are you set to take up any company of your choice, anywhere in the world no matter their size as your client?

May be you'll like to take up the government of your country as your client in business? Okay, pull up your sit, take a deep breathe because the secret that will make that happen is here.

First, lets look at the word unsolicited what does it mean? It means something not requested or asked for. So for a proposal to be unsolicited it means nobody has asked for it. That also means that it stands high chances of being rejected because nobody asked for it. As a matter of fact someone might even not give it a look.

Sometime ago I made a proposal I considered very wonderful to a bank. It's a pretty good idea. I was very proud of it and I thought, well no one could reject this. So I was patiently awaiting the reply to the proposal from the organization. Then after a while, I sent another proposal to the same company on another idea. One day, I got a call on my cell phone. The company asked to see me based on my proposal. Now the moment I heard that, I concluded it was the first one they were contacting me for.

I was about sending my marketing manager to them with necessary materials to defend the first proposal but hesitated.

When I got to their board room for the meeting, what was before me? The second proposal! Well, if it were you what will you do? I defended the proposal and closed the deal.

Then I pointed out to the chairman that I had sent a proposal earlier to the company. Do you know what? My proposal has not even been considered! Did it get to the chairman's table? Yes. But now under a pile of files!

Even though, it did not meet their needs when he went through it. But what if it went met their need? It was not even looked at. So the chances of closing a sale were not there because it remained an unexplored territory until I meet with the company. And they owe me no apologies because they did not request a proposal from me in the first place. This is the fate of most unsolicited proposals.

That's why I learnt everything I could about unsolicited proposals. It took me time, it took my sweat. I discovered the secret that makes it work and now I offer it to you.

Here is a fact about unsolicited proposal. Normally people read from people they know, and in most cases, the people you will be sending your unsolicited proposals to may not even know who you are. If you are listening to news for instance and they mentioned the name of the President of Nigeria, you may sure want to know what he has said or done. But if they mention a name you do not know, you may not be as interested as in the earlier case, except in a case when they mention something stricken about the person.

The media know this very well and take advantage of it. So they will report:

"President Buhari, signs health bill into law."
Then, "Man raped mother and daughter before husband."

You see in the first case what attracts you to the story is the President's name. In the second, though you don't know the man the bizarre nature of the story was what got your attention. They provoked your inquisitiveness which is natural in every human being. It's an interesting psychological phenomenon that works all the time and you will be learning how to use it to your own advantage in this book.

By the way what the media sends out is unsolicited proposals. No one asked them for their news; they just send them out hoping it will get some ones attention. Do they succeed? You answer!

What does that represent? To get your unsolicited proposal to win, you must learn all tools, tricks, the abcs and 123s of writing a wining proposal. A proposal no one can reject.

And   this   is   the   secret   that   make   it   work...

THE SEVEN HIDDEN SECRETS OF A WINNING IDEA PROPOSAL.

A beautiful idea landed me one day. So inspiring to me, I sat down right away and began putting it down on paper. Have you had that experience before?

I got down to work right away and made ready a wonderful proposal for a telecommunication giant in Lagos. A few days later, I bought my ticket and headed to Lagos. Moments later we were there.

I found my way to the company head office and joined other "travelers" on the elevator. I was headed for the 11th floor to meet the marketing manager of the corporation.

No response ever came from the company.

But my idea was pretty fine and great enough to make me millionaire. Why did it not work then?

Success is knowing how the world functions. The various systems or what the Greek will call *aion* has a way they work. When you try and did not get through it does not mean something is wrong with you or your idea. All you need do is get to study and understand the system you want to work. Simple enough isn't it?

Your idea might be wonderful but when you want to set it on course for success, this is your code...

1. Get to know your prospect
2. Define your intention specifically
3. Present with power
4. Align your thought with your intent
5. Sharpen your axe
6. Understand timing
7. Take the right action

Simple right? But also simple enough to make anybody loose. That's our task here: to explore the seven vital steps, you'll need to make your unsolicited proposal win.

CHAPTER 4

GET TO KNOW YOUR PROSPECT

"Now the Lord had said unto Abram, Get thee out of thy country, and from thy kindred, and from thy fathers house, unto a land that I will show thee. And I will make of thee a great nation and I will bless thee, and make thy name great, and thou shalt be a blessing. And I will bless them that bless thee, and curse him that curseth thee. And in thee shall all families of the earth be blessed" GENESIS 12: 1-3.

If you were Abraham, would you accept that proposal? To accept a proposal from someone you don't know, one condition is certain; it must address your specific need. The Bible did not tell us so much about who Abraham was before God made him the proposal. But the bible did tell us that Sarai, Abraham's wife was barren (vs 30) and that's very important.

For Sarai to have been described barren means that every hope was already lost about her conception, otherwise the bible would have said, "But Sarai was yet to conceive".

Now, you understand the trauma couples pass through if they have no kids. They can even do anything to have one.

Abram must have even offered sacrifices to his gods, for the scriptures let's us to know that he was a devoted man in his religion. That means he wanted a child really bad! He could pay any price for it and do anything for it. This is his hot spot, and any point that attacks that spot directly cannot be defeated! (Note that)

So note the first benefit, God offered Abram, "And I will make of you a great nation" Well, that connotes he will have children from whom the great nation would be manifested.

Again, notice the chronology of the generation from Genesis 11 and you will see that people were merely growing up, taking wives and then dying. There was no form of greatness and there was also no record of wealthy people in UR where Abram lived. No one was wealthy.

We notice this in vs 31 of Geneses 11 where they moved over to Haran under the leadership of their father, Terah.

There was no record of cattle, sheep or goat going with them. This shows us they were not rich people. So now look at the contents of God's proposal to Abram:

"And I will bless thee, and make thy name great, and thou shalt be a blessing." (Genesis 12:2) So you see Abram should be insane to reject this proposal. A proposal that promised to address all he has lived his life searching for.

Again, would you reject such a proposal if you were Abram?

To do well and make your proposal win, you will need to know your prospects very well. This is not just a casual knowledge, but accurate and comprehensive knowledge of your intending client or customer.

When you have a full knowledge of someone, you can be certain to help him or her. No doctor would be so insane as to begin prescription for a patient without first taking time to know the patient's present level of health and even in some cases, the past.

When you know a business, where they are, what they do, what they want to do and what they need, you can be most certain your proposal cannot be rejected. When you are bereaved of this basic information, you will be working based on guess work and your guesswork would most likely fail you. But when you work with precise knowledge, oh boy!

Okay, look at the story of the woman Jesus met in John 4.

First, Jesus got her attention. Jesus being a Jew should not speak with a Samaritan for they were enemies. This is important; you must get the attention of your intending client or customer before anything else.

After attention has been established, Jesus then gave her an analysis of her Nollywood kind of family life, "thou hast has five husband and he whom thou now hast is not thy husband" (John 4:18)

Jesus went a step further and shook her religious belief and at instance nullifying a mental attitude that represented a faith in an age long religious belief. "God is a Spirit and they that worship Him must worship Him in Spirit and in Truth. (vs 24)

The woman thought worship should be at specific place at some special times. Jesus maintained that worship is here and now.

To end the discussion and move on with her life, she said, "Well let's just leave the whole thing until the Messiah comes." Just like saying, well you are a nice guy, I love this proposal, but emmh, let's see what happens, and then the proposal is placed in the drawer and may be forgotten even.

So what did Jesus do? Tell her Okay, bye? No, not Jesus! He went all out, "I, that speak unto thee am He"

Jesus closed the sale and made the women an instant evangelist!

Again, what's the secret? Jesus knew her. He knew the deep questions in her mind and He addressed it, and won the woman over.

To do well, you must know the customer / client you intend to win. You must know who they are, what they are doing and what they want to do, where they are going and where they want to go. A certian man puts it this way succinctly put it, "with control, victory can be crafted by those with skill."

Barak Obama understood the heartbeat of the American people. He knew their yearning and utmost desire. It is the restoration of the original American Ideals; they call it *The American Dream.* That dream is unconsciously but consistently passed unto every child born in the United States. That's what the Americans truly wanted but not many have being bold enough to take up the mission.

On January 6, 1941 Franklin Delano Roosevelt, in his "The Four Freedoms," address to the U.S. Congress stated as follows:

"We look forward to a world founded upon four essential human freedoms.

The first is freedom of speech and expression — everywhere in the world.

The second is freedom of every person to worship God in his own way — everywhere in the world.

The third is freedom from want — which, translated into world terms, means economic understandings which will secure to every nation a healthy peacetime life for its inhabitants — everywhere in the world.

The fourth is freedom from fear — which, translated into world terms, means a worldwide reduction of armaments to such a point and in such a thorough fashion that no nation will be in a position to commit an act of physical aggression against any neighbor — anywhere in the world."

In their declaration of independence Thomas Jefferson stated:
When in the Course of human events it becomes necessary for one people to dissolve the political bands which have connected them

with another and to assume among the powers of the earth, the separate and equal station to which the Laws of Nature and of Nature's God entitle them, a decent respect to the opinions of mankind requires that they should declare the causes which impel them to the separation.

We hold these truths to be self-evident, that all men are created equal, that they are endowed by their Creator with certain unalienable Rights, that among these are Life, Liberty and the pursuit of Happiness.

Barak Obama understood all these and presented himself to the American people following the seven strange laws you are learning about and they elected him their president. He triumphed over the odds and broke the age long barrier of race in the United States to become the first black man to occupy the highest political position in the United States nay, the world.

Knowledge grants you control and control guarantees your victory. So do not be in a hurry to begin proposing. No, first take enormous time and be willing to also commit your resources to studying who your intending client or customers is.

Rather than make a futile effort of sending proposals which cannot win and then getting discouraged and exclaiming "it does not work", take out sometime to know who your client or customer is.

APPLICATION GUIDE

1. What is the name of the company?
2. When was it established?
3. What's the company vision and mission
4. Where is the head office located?
5. Who constitutes the board members and what are their experiences and qualifications?
6. What are they doing presently?
7. What have they done in the past?
8. What are their future forecasts?
9. What are the competitors of this company doing presently?
10. What percentage of the market were they sharing within the past five years?
11. What percentage of the market do they share presently?

I hope you did not hold your head and scream.

Comprehensive answers to those questions would help you produce a proposal that no one can say "no" to. When you have known who they are where they are going and even where their competitors are and where they are going, how can they say "no" to you?

Interestingly, it's not a big deal to gather all those information. We will be happy to help you. Simply email admin@fromideatomoneyproject.info

CHAPTER 5

DEFINE YOUR INTENTION PRECISELY

This is actually where it all begins. Before you write one word on paper first sit down and ask yourself, what do I really want? Knowing about a company is not enough, what do you really want to do with this knowledge?

Do you want to help them or do you want to take from them? Do you want to help them make more money or do you want to make more money with them? Do you want to create more customers for them or do you want to make them loose some of their customers? Do you want to add value to them or make them loose value? Sit down and ask yourself, what do I want to do with this company?

But, be sure of thus one thing, you can't expect your proposal to work when your mind is not connected to the very heart beat of the company. Remember, that they have a vision to fulfill. It is that vision that keeps them moving, that's why they stay late in the office, pay taxes, wake up early and even stay awake all night at times. In fact, that vision is them. If your proposal does not connect to that vision beyond the written words, forget it!

Even when you manage your way through at times, it will only be for a while. The reason is we are all spirit beings and we are all connected in the spirit realms. People call it intuition.

Back at the mind of the MD of Reality Bank is the vision to *provide financial services that will meet the specific need of all stakeholders in the spirit of excellence.*

This is his burning obsession, his passion, his love, and in fact, his entire life. He has been so much engrossed in this vision that he has staked his entire future on it. And here is a proposal on his desk from a man whose major concern is how to put some extra naira in his pocket.

Listen carefully my dear friend, forget it. Why?
Many wealthy men have purchased newspapers with the idea of advancing their personal fortunes, or bringing about some political action in which they have a private interest. Such newspapers

almost invariably fail... <u>The public has a sixth sense for detecting insincerity; they know instinctively when words ring true.</u>

Those words were written by Bruce Barton in 1925 and that's exactly true. You cannot build your idea on dishonest and expect to do well. You may get away with it at a few instances but you can NEVER have a lasting success.

The Fraudster Called Jacob

The name Jacob came from the Hebrew word *ya'ăqob* which means supplanter, one who takes the place or position of somebody by force or intrigue. Jacob's character eventually became consistent with his name.

Jacob took Esau's place by intrigue and paid with a life of hardship which included serving another man for fourteen years to get one woman. Think about it. It wasn't until he sought the LORD for help that his life got straightened up.

Your desires cannot counter that of your prospect and you expect to win. It does not matter that you win once or twice, for when the wind of justice blows you and your wicked idea will be no more. (Psalm 1:5) Look around you, learn from Enron, Lehman Brothers, Oceanic Bank etc and be wise.

No man can prosper his level of interest in the good of others. Albert Einstein said, *try to become not a man of success, but try rather to become a man of value*. How true! You cannot create value consistently and not heap success upon success. That's not going to happen.

Make up our mind to love and care and to support another man's vision with your entire mind for therein is the secret of creativity. Be driven by the desire to help your prospects win and you will find your way into their 'favorites' list.

When you have known a company and what to help them do better, you are simply opening your mind to ideas and creativity. You become like a vessel carrying the answers to ideas and creativity, a vessel carrying the answers to their prayers and longings of their heart and this way you cannot be rejected.

Here is one sure thing that would happen to you the moment you really make up your mind to help. First, you will start receiving interesting ideas about how to help and then the ideas will so much excite you that it will become a burning desire. This burning desire is what you require to stand against the odds and opposition that will necessarily come against you.

APPLICATION GUIDE

1. Meditate on the nation
2. Write what you know about the nation
3. What do think can be done to match the vision of the nation with reality
4. Think about it, talk about it to anyone who cares to listen but ignore and avoid the cynics
5. Propose that idea to your prospect.

This page is intentionally left blank

CHAPTER 6

PRESENT WITH POWER

There was a little city with few men in it. And a great king came against it and besieged it and built great bulwarks against it. But there was found in it a poor wise man, and he by his wisdom delivered the city. Yet no man [seriously] remembered that poor man. But I say that wisdom is better than might, though the poor man's wisdom is despised and his words are not heeded. Ecclesiastes 9:14-16(*Amplified*)

Why do you think the wise man was quickly forgotten? The answer is clear, he did not command power! The quality of your personality should reflect in everything about you. Did you ever hear that saying, *your dressing determines the way you are addressed?* How true? You might be the most insightful person on earth and the very solution that men seek, but if you don't present yourself with excellence you will be neglected.

The world does not have value for cheap materials. If you make you ideas appear cheap and unattractive nobody will want them. The idea that will turn into money will have to be properly packaged. The packaging inspires confidence in your prospects. It helps them make up their mind to try. This is a law and it applies to whatever you sale.

This does not suggest that you have to give people wrong impression about your idea. No, far from that. It simply means that you have to understand your idea and it's value to your prospect. You then present it from a position of importance knowing what benefits it will serve your prospect rather than as someone seeking assistance. Help your prospect see the value of your idea and never act like you are desperate. Don't act like you can't do without your prospect. No, present with power, act like many others are on the waiting list because they are indeed, just that you may not have met them.

Don't use cheap materials. Let everything associated with your idea be topnotch, that's a proof you respect the idea. You say that will be expensive. But *expensive* is a relative word. You only think something is expensive when you compare it with others in its class. This boils down to what you think about your idea in the first instance. Do you think you've got a world-class idea or do you think you've got an inferior stuff? You answer determines the level of commitment you give to your idea.

Donald Trump said he can spot a looser when he sees a man who has a *for sale* sign on a dirty car. I think that's true. I know how to spot a looser too, it's the man begging or forcing me to buy an idea he could not represent powerfully.

People will pay for your idea not because they want to help you but because they want to benefit from what you have. They want help and are hoping your idea will offer some, so you and your idea have to look like you can help.

Here's the best part of it, there's an inner awareness that attracts to you everything you require to present with power. It's not really in the quality of your packaging, as important as that is, it's in this inner awareness. Infact, this awareness will literarily compel you to present with power and the way to activate it is to change your disposition towards you and your idea. See, that you are seeking a job does not make you inferior to man that owns the business. You might be all he needs to move to another level, so he needs you. That you are applying for a contract does not make you less important than the man awarding the contract irrespective of whether or not there are 20,000 of you applying for the same contract. Recognize that your idea is God's gift to make you relevant, so treasure them. If you God has now trusted you with this idea, have respect for it and present it with power. The one who knows this is the one whose ideas will turn to money. Nothing can stop the idea of the man who presents with power.

So the packaging of the proposal should be strong and good enough to convince your prospect that this will be valuable to him.

It should be confidently presented in simple but matured way to convince your prospect that he needs it. If your proposal appears like a beggar, chances are that even if it finds its way to the intending prospects table and even if it does, it will still end up in a trash can.

APPLICATION GUIDE

1. Write professionally but simple enough too so you can be understood. The correct professional language regarding the area you are proposing must be evident in the proposal. Every profession has dictions, use them intelligently to spice up your work.

2. Use 1.5 line spacing.

3. Use, arial, tribucent MS, times new romans, georgia or similar fort styles. But make sure the font is simple

4. Use font size 10 – 12

5. Request a call, don't just some like you are hoping the company calls.

This page is intentionally left blank

CHAPTER 7

ALIGN YOUR THOUGHT WITH YOUR INTENT

Solomon did not say *as he thinketh in his heart so shall he have,* in Proverbs 23:7. No, he said *as he thinketh in his heart so is he.* That means the man will eventually become a revelation of his thoughts. What does that mean? Your outer world of experience is an exact reflection of your inner world of thought. Your outer world is just an expression of what's going on in your thoughts.

You cannot really win an idea you don't believe in. In the truest sense on life no man can win beyond the level of his conviction. Is that simple. Except you are 100% persuaded that you will win, you cannot win. If you think that you will loose, you have already lost, if you think the company will steal your idea and give another person the contract, oh they have already done it. Anyhow you think it is, that is just exactly how it stands. Your thought is your position.

Actually, whether or not your ideas will work lies within you because your whole world exists as thoughts in your mind.

There is the story of a man who wanted to be a business associate of Thomas Edison. A poor man he was. So poor he hadn't money to pay his far to Edison's office.

Physically there was nothing to behold of him, except for the thought of victory in his mind.

Finally, he arrived at Edison's office and stood before him, where he boldly declared his intention. Not for Edison to consider him for a job, or to see how he could help him but to accept him simple as his new business partner. Though physically there was nothing about him but his thoughts were those of a king! He never at anytime gave up on his convictions to become Edison's business partner. It did not happen overnight, but he sure made it.

So I tell you thoughts are things. A saying goes this way, "seeing is believing" and but that's not true. The time you win is not when you get an answer; rather it is when you believe it. So I say to you believing is seeing, as the Paul wrote, *while we look not at things which are seen but at things which are not seen* (2 Corinthians 4:18)

There are so many things which exist that cannot be seen with your optical eyes. If you must wait to see everything before you do something, you will never get started. For example you knew radio waves exist even though you cannot see that with your eyes, so you went ahead and bought a radio set. You knew wireless phone network exist before you bought your cell phone. You did not wait to see the network with your optical eyes. You just believed and when you did, you bought the phone and saw the network. Do you get that?

Your thoughts must be stayed on the success of your proposal even before you write a word on paper. Don't just send out your proposal to see whether or not it will work. No, know what you do not want.

1. You don't want to get ignored by the company.
2. You don't want to wait forever without response of any sort.

3. You don't want to waste your precious time laboring over a project that will never work. No you don't. Do you?

Now you know what you don't want, carefully define what you do want.

1. You want your proposal to be answered.
2. Not only answered you want the company to do business with you.
3. You want the confidence, the improved self-image, the fame, the money and the good life it will offer you.

That's it. You know it.

Now remember, as a man thinketh in his heart ...if this is what you want, it must more than any other thing occupy your mind. You must meditate on it. Notice I said meditate.

Do that to the point it begins to come out of your month. To the point you are so certain about your success you can tell it to everyone you see. As you do this your thought vibration moves out and attract to itself the reality of your thought. Your whole world exists as thoughts in your mind.

Never forget that. The beautiful instruction given to Joshua in Joshua 1:8 would so much help here. God said to Joshua, you shall meditate on the book of the law so you'll observe to do according to all that's written therein then THOU SHALL MAKE THY WAY PROSPEROUS AND THOU SHALL HAVE GOOD SUCCESS!

Did you see that? The success of your idea has to consume you. It has to be a crystal clear image in your mind if you want it to work. Get convinced and get excited about your idea, talk about it with conviction, soon enough that picture only you sees will become visible to everyone else.

APPLICATION GUIDE

1. Write down the success story of your proposal.
2. Go to some quite place where you can be alone.

3. Begin to read aloud to yourself the written story of your success

4. Fix all your attention on it as you do that.

5. Keep reading until you sweat and the passion of victory is rushing down your spine.

6. Remain in this state.

CHAPTER 8

SHARPEN YOUR AXE

There is only one short cut to success - get educated. -BRIAN SHER.

Remember: The duller the ax the harder the work; Use your head: The more brains, the less muscle.-ECCLESIASTES 10:10 (Message)

Become an expert in your field. Interestingly, education is beyond completing a course in school. The purpose of education is to give you a new awareness, it is much more than being certified by an institution.

Bottom line? It's an everyday thing and it last a lifetime. Oh how often people loose opportunities because they lack the proficiency required! To be proficient means that you are skillful in the command of fundamentals deriving from practice and familiarity. And this is only possible through personal capacity development. Make no mistakes about it, there are boundless opportunities in the world for the man who is skillful at his work.

Don't propose to anybody to do a job you do not know so much about. Even if you succeed with one person, you will park up a lorry load of failure.

This will get you discouraged and subsequently, frustrated. Do you understand?

Go for training; attend seminars, buy books in your area of interest. Constantly update your knowledge. Be willing to commit your time and resources to acquiring more and more knowledge in your field.

Your competence increases as your knowledge increases. Competence is what makes you a master and who can say no when a master shows up? Individuals and nations are in search of people with mastery to help them realize their interest. That's what Kings search for. Nebuchadnezzar was very specific in his demand in Daniel 1:4: *Children in whom was no blemish, but well favoured, and skilful in all wisdom, and cunning in knowledge, and understanding science, and such as had ability in them to stand in the king's palace.*

In Proverbs 12:24 Solomon said, *the hand of the diligent shall bear rule: but the slothful shall be under tribute.* To be diligent means to be persistent and hard-working in doing something. But hard work only produces its best results when a man is competent. If you can't drive a car you can't be diligent at driving one. So you need to be the best at what you do and the only way is through consistent training.

What are you known for? Who are you? What do you do? You must become so good at what you do that you cannot be rejected, so good that you cannot be ignored, so good that your name will become synonymous with it. And the stair case to that is sharpening your axe. Be the best at what you do!

APPLICATION GUIDE

1. Go get all the books you can lay your hand on concerning the business you do or would want to do.

2. Decide the specific amount you will keep down each mouth for seminars.

3. Get a coach in your area. There' so many things you can learn from another man's experience.

4. Make friends that have genuine interest in the business you do.

5. Give more of your time to developing yourself than any other thing.

CHAPTER 9

UNDERSTAND TIMING

You may end up giving a company an idea for the future if you don't understand timing. Most likely they will not pay for it. Your proposal may look nice but just get to your prospect either when they no longer have need for it or don't need it yet.

May be this story will help.
I landed a beautiful idea that will help NOKIA so much in marketing their products.

Good a thing I had known one of their top managers through my relationship with another company where he had worked. So he gave me the direct line of the marketing manager and I forwarded my proposal directly to him.

Did they like my idea? Yes. Did the business work? No.

Why? The time was just wrong. The idea was nice but got to them at the wrong time. You must understand timing.

I returned, and saw under the sun, that the race is not to the swift, nor the battle to the strong, neither yet bread to the wise, nor yet riches to men of understanding, nor yet favour to men of skill; but time and chance happeneth to them all. - Ecclesiastes 9: 11

Did you see that? In fact The Living Bible puts it in a better perspective for us. It rendered that verse this way …it *is all by chance by happening to be at the right place at the right time.* Even if you are of the right place, you will also need to be there not before or after, but at the right time.

A certain man puts it this way, *Generally, an executive can survive within the power structure of his organization. It is a matter of taking appropriate actions and providing adequate service to his constituency. But when an executive dominates a situation, it is because he creates opportunity and understands timing, it is a matter of showing strength and apparent of weakness, reality and illusion. Competitors do not know what to defend against. When the speed of a diving falcon breaks the neck of its prey; it is due to precise timing.*

Success in life and business depends on being at the right place at the right time, but when is the right time? How can you know the right time to send that proposal? Which time is right?

May be this story will help make it clearer. There was a man called Moses in the bible. The way one that led the Israelites out of Egypt, you remember him? Okay!

Now Moses knew he was to be the deliverer of the children of Israel from their bondage in Egypt, (Acts 7:25) so what did he do with such a beautiful Vision? Well, he thought he was going to kill the Egyptians one after another, so he went to work right away! He did not know that God had already appointed for the children of Israel to live in Egypt 430 years. What was the effect? Failure in fact, he had to run away and remained in a foreign land until the due time.

Consider this also. It's being said that before 1880 few American homes had bathtubs or even running water. The companies which tried to sale bathtub then didn't make much money out of it. In fact some states placed taxes on the companies. One state passed a law making it illegal to sale bathtubs. It was the wrong time.

You see that? Your proposal may be good but until the time is ripe it will not work.

Can you understand the times? 1Chronicles 12:32 talked about the children of Issachar, which were men that had understanding of the times to know what Israel ought to do. Because they knew what the people should do, they gave them the chance.

Don't let the pursuit of money blind you. People may not care that you are hungry or broke, but they will care when you have the answers they seek. They way to receive ideas consistent with the time is to focus on creating value; we've talked about this before. When you are focused on creating value, you open yourself to ideas consistent with the time.

APPLICATION GUIDE

1. Know your prospect very well in terms of the values they provide.
2. Regularly update your knowledge about their activities.
3. Monitor the activities of your prospects competitors and make forecasts.

CHAPTER 10

TAKE THE RIGHT ACTION

There aren't many companies where leaders would produce a new operating plan for a major part of the company in ten days. More often there'd be a lot of talk and off-site conferences but no action. - RAM CHARAN

How true that is! It's not just in the planning and meditation. It's in the execution. That's where the big payoff is. All we've talked about will accomplish nothing if you don't learn to take action when your chance opens.

Go all out, spare no bridges, and give it all it takes. You may need to knock more than once before a door opens for you. That should not be a problem. Stay on your game and be on top of it. This is your game; you can't afford to give up on it just because someone said no.

Now, you've done all the home work you need to do. You know your prospect; you are filed with confidence because you are proficient. When the chance is granted your idea will make a difference and you think the time is here. Now you have to take action. This is your game and you are going to win.

In 1928 Bruce Barton wrote *one never knows, when he enters an elevator or tears open an envelope or picks up the telephone, what new trick of fortune may be about to be played. Every day is a new series of adventures; around the next corner may lie the event that will change a whole career.* Every proposal has the potential to turn your ideas into money. Never undermine the power of your proposals; they can change a whole generation. So send them out to the right people. The proof that you believe in your idea is that you sell it to people. If you don't, somebody eventually will.

Consider Mozart, Austrian composer, who is considered one of the most brilliant and versatile composers ever. He worked in all musical genres of his time, wrote inspired works in each genre, and produced an extraordinary number of compositions

He wrote the world's greatest music, yet died penniless. Those who followed him, who knew how to turn ideas to money, grew wealthy by marketing his works.

Your idea can be the best and the very thing the world seeks, yet except you let people know what you can do for them, you'll struggle through life and many whose life would have been made easier because of your idea will live without it because you failed to take action.

Your success is guaranteed. You are not the first to attempt. Many have done that and won, you too will win. If you've followed through with the secrets we have shared in this book you already have the tools you require to turn your ideas to money.

With these secrets you can sure turn any idea to money, but there's more...

This page is intentionally left blank

CHAPTER 11

HOW TO MAKE PEOPLE LOVE YOUR IDEA

But if we walk in the light, as he is in the light, we have fellowship one with another – 1 John 1:7

One of the interesting ironies of life is that people are preoccupied. They are concerned about themselves, their money, their family, their money. They are not really thinking about you and your ideas. As long as they are preoccupied that way, you cannot make an impression on their mind except you speak their mental preoccupation. And except you make a positive impression on them, there's no sale.

It's nothing wrong, life is designed that way. John in his first epistle 1:7 said the same thing about God. He said, *if we walk in the light, as he is in the light, we have fellowship one with another.* To walk in the light as He is in the light means to operate in His consciousness. He said when we do, we have fellowship (Greek: *koinōnia*) with Him.

Koinoᾱia translated **fellowship** also means **communication.** That means to communicate your ideas to your prospects and get them hear you, you must uncover their mental preoccupation.

This is what hypnosis will help you achieve.

However, I know several people associate hypnosis with evil basically because they don't know what hypnosis is. Since you may be probably unclear as to what hypnosis really is, let me offer some explanations.

First of all hypnosis never removes choice. You can't be made to do something under hypnosis that you didn't already want to do while fully awake. Hypnosis simply breaks through your preoccupation to your inner awareness. You said 'yes' to a hypnotic offer because you already wanted the offer, hypnosis simply made it easy for you.

Secondly, hypnosis is not evil. It is used by dentists, doctors, and psychologists to help individuals get what they truly want in life. The American Medical Association endorsed it since the 1950s. Anyone who still thinks hypnosis is evil is simply being ignorant.

I see hypnosis as anything that holds your attention. A TV show, or book, is a type of hypnosis. So is an attractive lady, or sales pitch, or infomercial. I don't mean controlling minds but rather entertaining them.

Here's the fact: Hypnosis is just another tool. It does not control people and it does not give God-like powers to anyone. In turning your idea to money, it gives you an edge, but if you use it to try to sell a worthless idea, it won't help you at all. It gives you a unquestionable advantage over the competition but not over the client.

Hypnosis will help you get and hold attention. It also makes you a much better communicator.

You need it to effectively turn your ideas into money. After all the missing link between your idea and its realization lies in your ability to effectively communicate it to those that need it.

Study shows that within 24 hours, people are hypnotized

approximately 39 times most assuredly; they did not even know it. What do you think happens to you when your favorite show comes up on TV?

There you were surrounded by all manner of distractions of all sorts-phone ringing, dogs barking, children playing, and all that-yet because something good was on, you were spellbound, concentrating only on the drama unfolding on that relatively small fraction of your environment-the TV screen.

You are also effectively hypnotized when you're surfing the internet, when you are engrossed in a book, when you are lost in a thought or even when an attractive person walks by, or you see an attractive car, house or anything. Do you understand?

Simply put, hypnosis means living in a state of *altered consciousness*

What does this have to do with turning ideas to money?

Like I showed you earlier, you can't get attention except you breakthrough your prospect's mental preoccupation. When a person is in this altered state of consciousness, that is having his/her full attention focused on just one thing that person is highly suggestible.

This means that the person is more likely to accept and act upon, suggestions that you make.

In terms of proposing your ideas it means that you can zero in on your prospects altered state and deliver hypnotic suggestions that would induce them to say yes to whatever you are proposing easily. They can be compelled to *obey* whatever you suggest as though they were mesmerized into submission. More importantly is that they will find your suggestions irresistible.

How can you apply hypnosis to communicate your message more precisely?

Paul, A Master Hypnotist.

So Paul, taking his stand in the centre of the Areopagus, spoke as follows: Men of Athens, I perceive that you are in every respect remarkably religious.

For as I passed along and observed the things you worship, I found also an altar bearing the inscription, 'TO AN UNKNOWN GOD.' The Being, therefore, whom you, without knowing Him, revere, Him I now proclaim to you. GOD who made the universe and everything in it--He, being Lord of Heaven and earth, does not dwell in sanctuaries built by men.

Nor is He ministered to by human hands, as though He needed anything--but He Himself gives to all men life and breath and all things.

He caused to spring from one forefather people of every race, for them to live on the whole surface of the earth, and marked out for them an appointed span of life and the boundaries of their homes; that they might seek God, if perhaps they could grope for Him and find Him. Yes, though He is not far from any one of us.

For it is in closest union with Him that we live and move and have our being; as in fact some of the poets in repute among yourselves have said, 'For we are also His offspring.'

Since then we are God's offspring, we ought not to imagine that His nature resembles gold or silver or marble, or anything sculptured by the art and inventive faculty of man.

Those times of ignorance God viewed with indulgence. But now He commands all men everywhere to repent, seeing that He has appointed a day on which, before long, He will judge the world in righteousness, through the instrumentality of a man whom He has pre-destined to this work, and has made the fact certain to every one by raising Him from the dead. .

When they heard Paul speak of a resurrection of dead men, some began to scoff. But others said, 'We will hear you again on that subject.'

So Paul went away from them. A few, however, attached themselves to him and believed, among them being Dionysius a member of the Council, a gentlewoman named Damaris, and some others. (Acts 17:-22-34) (WNT)

Did you notice how Paul hypnotized the people as he made that proposal? That's what Paul did .He is a Master Hypnotist.

To really appreciate what Paul did, let us look at the case very objectively.

1. The setting:

This incident happened in Athens, the capital of Attica, and the chief seat of Grecian learning and civilization during the golden period of the history of Greece.

You of course know that the world's famous Philosophers Socrates, Plato, Aristotle and the rest of them are all Greek. Democracy, the philosophy that is adjudged best system of government which up till today dominates the world came from there. Are you there?

"Seeing that Jews demand Miracles and Greeks go in search of wisdom" (1Cor. 1:22) WNT

2. The audience and the subject:
Then certain philosophers of the Epicureans, and of the Stoicks, encountered him – Acts 17:18

Epicureans believe that the world was not made by any deity, or with any design, but came into its being and form, through a unexpected concourse of atoms, of various sizes and magnitude, which met, and mixed-up, and cemented together, and so formed the world; and that the world is not governed by the providence of God; for though they do not deny the being of God, yet he thought it below his notice, and beneath his dignity to concern himself with its affairs.

The Stoicks regarded God and the world as power, and its manifestation matter as being a passive ground, in which dwells the divine energy. The morality of stoicism is essentially based on pride and they believe the world will end in what they call *cosmical ruin*

So they saw Paul as *a setter forth of strange gods* (Acts 17: 18)

3. Their perception of Paul:

What has this beggarly babbler to say? (Acts 17:18)

That's how they saw him. Not as an authority whom they should listen to but as a beggarly babbler.

This was the setting, this was the situation.

So how was he even able to get a hold of their attention? Why didn't they walk away in the middle of the presentation? Not only was he able to hold their attention, he even won over some people to his side! Paul must be an incredible person.

So let us now analyze that proposal of his and see how he played the tricks.

Paul Hypnotized Them!

First, notice how Paul began. "Men of Athens, I perceive that you are in every respect remarkably religious." That was his very first statement. This got their attention. They liked it their faces lit up with smiles. They have been complemented. No one can resist the power of complement. (Note that) He first recognized something good about them and praised them.

That was also Jesus' strategy. Jesus is a master hypnotist. In the first chapter of John verses 45-50(WNT), a man known as Nathaniel was introduced to Jesus. Hitherto, Nathaniel had said nothing good could come out of Nazareth. He did not believe Jesus was the Christ; He was only coming to prove that Jesus was not.

So what did The LORD do? He paid him first of all, a compliment. Jesus said of him "Look! Here is a true Israelite, in whom there is no deceitfulness!"

The moment Jesus said this, He lost his defenses. Jesus pushed him out of control with his complement.

"How do you know me?" Nathaniel asked. "Before Philip called you" said Jesus, "when you were under the fig-tree I saw you."

"Rabbi, "cried Nathaniel, "You are the Son of God, you are Israel's King!"

Did you see how Jesus hypnotized Nathaniel with His complement and got him to say YES to his proposal?

That's the same strategy Paul began with. The moment praised them for their extra religiosity, he got their attention.

"For as I passed along and observed the things you worship, I found also an altar bearing the inscription, "TO AN UNKNOWN GOD" "The being, therefore, whom you, without knowing Him, revere, Him I now proclaim to you." (Vs 23)

"Oh! He is not even talking about a strange God", they must have thought, and that was the exact objective he wanted to achieve. This brought them together. He got agreement with them. They were not opposing themselves anymore. They were friends. This is called agreement. Jesus said "agree with thine adversary quickly." When you agree with your prospect, he opens up himself to you. It is a lot easier to persuade a man that believes in you than someone who does not. Infact, if you must persuade anybody you must agree with him first.

That's what Paul did, and the moment he achieved that he held them attentive as he intelligently presented them with the facts that will compel them to believe his message.

Gradually, he condemned their worship of graven images and before ever they could think about that to oppose him, he quoted their own poets as his authority, "As certain also of your own poets have said, for we are also his offspring" (vs 28)

At this point he has awakened the side of them that reasons. They have begun questioning the faith now "May be he is right, we are wrong." They must have thought.

Then Paul presented the main point of his idea. He told them about the resurrection from the dead.

What was the result? Some believed right away, others said they will like to hear more of his message and some laughed at him. Was that proposal successful? The answer is a resounding 'yes!' That's the same strategy you must apply. If it worked for Paul, it will work for you.

HOW TO HYPNOTIZE ANYONE

How do I apply hypnosis to get a company hire me? Someone asked. How do I get someone open account with my bank so I can meet my target using hypnosis? Another person asked. Yet a young woman asked, can I use hypnosis to get a young man interested in a relationship with me?

First understand you cannot use hypnosis to get someone do what he/she does not already want to do. You can only use it to help someone do what he/she wants but may be not aware of. You use hypnosis to eliminate the thoughts that may obstruct your idea in the mind of your prospect.

Now I want you to know here is that the hypnosis or trance that I'm describing here is not what in psychological terms is called *somnambulism* one, during which one is deep asleep but conscious of spoken words. It's more of what is called *waking hypnosis,* during which they are alert and aware; their eyes are open, but their minds are focused on something other than what is present with them

.

It was Wesley Wells who coined the term *waking trance* was coined in 1924 and it refers to the concentration of attention on something. It means being hyper focused on subject to the exclusion of everything else

Everyone Hypnotized!

Everyone at any time is always hypnotized by something. They are all in a trance. They are not thinking about you and your ideas no matter what your idea might be. They are thinking about them. They are thinking about their job, their money, their family, their car, their house. It's always their, their, their not you!

The first step in using hypnosis to get someone buy from

you, employ you, go out on a date with you or do anything for you is to know what their current trance is and then meet them there. What are they focused on presently? Except you understand this you will get offended at people for no reason. This is because the people you talk to don't hear you except you talk about what they are focused on. This is your first job.

Getting this done is not difficult when you master the skill but to the ignorant it's work. To determine what people are focused on you'll have to be a very intelligent observer. Know this, people cannot hide their thoughts, but you'll need to understand how to focus on people to hear what they are truly saying beyond the level of their awareness. How do you do that?

Pay attention to the stories they tell. When you get people to tell you a story you'll decode their trance, all you need is pay good attention to their language. Notice their choice of words and you can determine with accuracy where they are mentally. People reveal a lot of valuable information in their stories which they will otherwise not say in straight forward questions. The reason is, in their stories, their emotions are involved especially and emotions are more powerful than reasoning.

Listen to their complaints: In complaints people express their discontent or unhappiness about a situation and they rarely censor themselves when they do this. As they talk about what they don't like, it quickly helps to determine what they would prefer.

Value their questions. Questions are not solely requests for information. They're vehicles for expressing interest. Though the specific interests are sometimes disguised, the language (and by this I don't mean English or Italian) will clearly help you to see the intention behind the questions. What does this mean?

I Hope This Is Not A Religious Program?

I met a pretty young lady at a business center and opened a conversation with her the moment I realized she's written a book. This was close to my book presentation, so as the discussion progressed I handed her a copy of my book presentation invitation card. She admired it as I hoped she would and gave me a smile. Then the smile seemed to die right away. I got concerned. Have I done something wrong?

I wondered. Then she asked, I hope this is not a religious program? Do I look like a religious person? I responded. Well, I just wanted to know, because people now use different tricks to lure people to their religion.

The title of my book was *How To Make Your Ideas Work.* Nothing about it appeared religious. Why was this young lady concerned about religion? Again, the answer is simple, she as every other person is preoccupied. By that question she simply unveiled her current trance to me. This woman has some religious insecurity. She doesn't want to give a chance to the possibility of embracing another faith. Anything with a religious content will put her off. That was her preoccupation. I decoded it through that simple question; *I hope this is not a religious program?*

If you will learn to pay attention to the choice of words your prospects use as they express themselves, you'll definitely uncover their trance and met them there before you can lead them to where you want to.

Let me conclude this chapter like this. Find out what people have on their minds and connect with them there. You can always break their preoccupation with a shocking statement or action (or gift), but you can make friends with the faster if you merge with their dominant thoughts and concerns.

From there, they will follow your lead. But understanding has to come first. Remember, people buy only from people they know, they like, and they respect.

CHAPTER 13

HOW MARKETERS RULE THE WORLD!

For centuries psychologists have studied how people buy. Research after research, study after study has revealed a certain pattern. Anyone who successfully sold any idea used this secret principle.

In a while you will be discovering exactly what this secret is and how to effectively use it to your own success.

But first ask yourself, Why did you buy this book and most of all why have you read this far? Before you try to answer, let me give it to you...

You bought the book and has read this far because it got your **attention**, **interested** you, aroused your **desire** and thus stimulated your **action**. That's the secret fomular marketers have used for centuries to rule the world and make men and women buy and now you can learn how to do the same

Here's the fomular in a nutshell -
Attention, Interest, Desire, Action. (AIDA)

ATTENTION:

That's the first test you must pass. Your proposal has to get my attention before I can open it. This is because people are inundated with so many documents every day, beginning with bill boards to fliers and newspapers, TV commercials, and a whole lot of others.

This means your headline must be hypnotically compelling, if you want anyone to keep reading. It must get attention and suspense. Someone has got to desire to know more just by reading the heading; his head should get surging with emotions. Fill his mind with a movie, get him stretching his neck, Are you there?

So how do you make your headline or subject to hold attention? Simple, just take the following steps:

STRUCTURE YOUR HEADLINE AS A QUESTION AND PUT THEM IN PARENTHESIS.

Research and experience has shown that headlines or subjects structured this way gets increased readership by at least 15%.

Examples:

"Would You Like To Discover How To Get More People Open Account With Your Bank?"
This will definitely get the attention of a banker especially someone in marketing. If he must keep his job and climb the corporate ladder, he needs this.

"Who Else Wants To Get A Contract With The Federal Government?"
What do you think about that? Someone will at the least glace through that headline not just because it is structured as a question but because it also addresses one of the most powerful emotions. Can you identify that? It is money. More on this shortly.

"Are You A Real Man?"

Is there any man who can resist the power of that question? None! Structured this way, you'll get attention. Let's examine them even more closely…

First, I structured them as a question. You wanted to answer those questions. Right?

Second, I built in your personal desires into my questions. The first talked about money. The second also talked about money and third talked about personal value. People don't buy products and services, they buy the emotions which the offer suggest to them.

"Want To Look Beautiful?" The woman answers yes in her mind and sits back to watch the advertorial coming on the screen. But really when she thinks about beauty what does she want? Just beauty for the sake of it? No, she's thinking about the attractiveness to then opposite sex. I know there could be exceptions due to upbringing and philosophy, but this is usually the case.

"Would You Like To Discover How To Get More People Open Account With Your Bank?" The banker picks up the proposal to study it. He wants more customers. But for what purpose? He's thinking about the money it represents, the power and influence that comes from being recognized as the biggest bank in the world. That's what he's looking for.

Remember, people buy emotion. So when you frame your headlines think beyond your product to the emotional satisfaction they provide. Focus on that and make it as obvious as it can be.

You must construct your own headline the same way if you want to get attention. I said you have to do that.

Again it's smart to write the first letters of your headline in the upper case, otherwise you **bolden** them. This makes them stand out of the body and hence catch attention. Do well also to <u>underline</u> your important words, especially those that carry the key benefit (the emotional satisfaction) to your clients.

Here are some phrases you can use in phrasing your headline:

- How Seriously…
- Who Else…

- Would You Finally...
- What Is...
- Are you finally...
- Do you think...
- What Would Happen If...

Here are other words that work. They do not take the structure of questions but they trigger off questions in your mind:

- Discover...
- Revealed...
- How To...
- Simple Ways...
- Secrets To...

Here are other ways to structure your headline to get attention:

SPEAK IN PARABLES

Use stories that create suspense in people's mind. Get them wanting to know more. Jesus did it and held the attention of His listeners and you absolutely should.

Examples:

"How A Little Cartoon Can Attract More Guest To Your Hotel, Everyday."

"Discover War Secrets That Can Increase Your Company ROI Almost Rapidly"

Did you notice that in each of those instances you felt hungry for details? Yes, that's because I held you in suspense with my stories. Don't you know human beings like 'gossips'? That's why the media inundates you with that on the TV, Radio and Papers. People like stories, so if you want to get and even hold their attention, give them what they want. Stories, yes, use it to your advantage.

MAKE A BIG CLAIM

Usually you will have to blow your own trumpet. Who will do it better than you?

Donald Trump is famous for making big claims. He will announce that he is erecting the tallest building in New York. When he does he gets attention. The media carries it, people get to talk about it and that way spreading his idea for him.

P T Barnum knew the same trick and used it to his advantage. He once named his museum *Barnum's American Museum* crowds flowed in to his museum.

The LORD, Jesus Christ was very good at that and used it effectively. Of course you will bet He must have. Is He not the embodiment of all wisdom? Once He said, destroy this temple and in three days I will raise it up" John 2:19. That got the attention of everyone. It has always worked and you need to start using it today.

Make big claims and you will get attention but also be ready to defend your claims otherwise people will get disappointed and begin to take you unserious

INTEREST:

That's the second important rule. "What's in it for me?" The purpose of a proposal is to show a client how you could be of help to him. How you could solve a problem for him and make his life better. The moment, you get his attention; this is the thing he looks out for. And if you must hold his attention, you must show him right from the outset what's in it for him. Did you get that?

Some people spend their time talking about issues that has no way of benefitting the prospect. Some talk about their experiences and qualifications. Others concentrate on talking about the number of office locations they have, their oversea partners, their expensive equipment and all those nonsense. They think that will get the prospect to jump up and scream and then start rolling the contract or job for them right away. But it is not so.

What your prospect wants is the conviction that you can do it better for him and nothing else. Do that for him and save him the time. Your qualifications, experiences, oversea advantages and all that will make no meaning to your prospect unless you are able to connect them to how they will benefit him. In most case he does not care if you are monkey, a gorilla or a human being, the concern he has is, 'can this person really help me?' For instance, do you really care how the ATM machine by the corner works? All you want is to get cash whenever you insert your card. Isn't it?

Listen, when your clients say no to your proposals it's because you were unable to get them convinced. (Note That!) When you are unable to close the deal, the simple reason is because you could not communicate the interest of your client to him, logically and effectively. Never forget that. Customers and clients never really say no to you or your services or products. No, just that they did not see themselves represented in the proposal.

So here's my advice: talk in terms of the benefits of you product or service to your client, not how wonderful your product or service or even you and your company is. You might just end up getting your prospect bored and may be even angry, He may even think that you are braggadocios and hence you loose the deal.

As you propose be sure to imagine the objections your prospect might have and treat them in your presentation. Agree with them on those areas and assure them they are not making any mistake.

Example:

I understand that you may be skeptical. You may be wondering if this is the typical long sales letter full of hype and promises that someone can't keep. I respect that, but I want to tell you...

Because I want to make 100% sure that you are happy with your purchase...

Because I want to make 100% sure that you'll see results from your efforts...

Because I want you to become highly successful in marketing your business...

Because I want to make sure that you feel 100% comfortable with your purchase today, here's my promise to you:

If for any reason whatsoever you feel that the information in Definitive Guide To Home Business wasn't worth at least 10 times the $97 ONLY $47 you paid, I'll gladly refund you the full investment, no questions asked.

And you can even have a full 365 days to try all of the strategies you'll learn in all of your materials.

That's lifted from one of my proposals on my book, 'Definitive Guide To Home Business' still on sale. That was the secret of Paul used that made him very effective.

Look at that his proposal in Acts 17 again. For one moment he did not talk about himself or the superiority of his faith. He concentrated on his prospects and the benefits they will get by becoming together as he is.

When he felt their minds may wonder away and they begin to oppose him, he quoted their own poets as his authority and that they could not resist. "As certain also of your own poets have said, for we are also his offspring" (Acts 17 vs 28)

Are you surprised he was that effective? This is the secret he walked with and now you can take advantage of the same.

DESIRE:

Understand this, you must create the desire for me to go for your product or service, if you want me to respond. You've gotta get my passion activated. Did you get that?

How do you get this one done? Well, this is very psychological but simple to apply. You only need to concentrate on arousing my emotions to get me passionate. How do you do that?

To do this you must understand what I really want. The reason people buy cars is not the car itself, but the comfort, the convenience and the feelings that goes with it. So if you talk about a beautiful red jeep that I should own, that may not really move me even though I would like to have one.

But if you begin talking to me about how the jeep moves at a tremendous spend of 380KM/Hour. How the tires are made of superior rubber newly discovered in Africa that no sharp object can penetrate and in fact how I would not have need to change tires ever. How it has a special camera that can monitor my office from wherever I might be, How the President of Ghana uses it for his official functions and yet I could get it for just about the same rate as 2013 model *LandRover* jeep I intend to buy, then you might be getting close to getting a Yes from me because now you are appealing to my ego which is a strong emotion in everyman.

Same thing goes for any product or service you may be selling now or ever want to sale. Tell me how the new current account package of your bank will save me from COT and how my funds are secured by the huge financial strength of your bank amounting to over $20,000 000 in shareholders fund and save me with the details of how your own bank is better that so-so-and so.

What am I saying? To get your prospects desire your product or service, saturate your proposal with the benefits to him. Help him create a drama and make him the key actor. Create the picture of his improved life just because he said 'yes' to your offer. Who doesn't like a better life? If you do that they cannot just say no.

Consider these case studies:

Come to think of it, don't you think you owe it to yourself to take advantage of this amazing opportunity before the offer closes?
If you allow your *brain* to deceive you and let you make a pass on this now, you may not have the chance of ever seeing such an offer anywhere again!

I can assure you with the certainty of one exchanging GSM numbers with God that you owe it up to yourself 100% to say "YES" today.

What you are getting is a secured passport to the wealth and happiness you have long sought. This is a thing you'll get now and it will forever change your life.

You know that feeling you get when you've really achieved something? That warm sensation in your stomach, the confidence to walk down the street knowing you're more successful than your neighbors, colleagues and friends, someone that your family looks up to...

OK, picture feeling like that 356 days a year. Imagine if you no longer had to worry about how your boss feels about you, if you don't keep awake all night thinking about salary raise or government policy about importation because you have a completely automated money maker working overtime just for you.

Well let me tell you something, you've never been closer to changing your life, all that remains is for you to reach out and grab it...and I will suggest, do it now

That's an excerpt from one of my proposals.

Did you notice the drama I created in your mind as you were reading through that? That's what you must also do.

ACTION:

That's the fourth of the principle and it is here so many people miss the whole thing. A proposal without a call to action isn't a proposal at all. You just can propose without calling people to take action.

So many people think it is a sign of weakness to call for action. So they say, 'Well, I have presented the facts, if somebody wants to buy, he would.' So they would not call to action and leave it that way.

No, tell people to take the action you want them to. If you want them to call you, tell them to. If you want them to buy now, tell them to. Don't just think they know it and so will know what to do.

Listen to me in the most cases they don't, so tell them! I often experience this with business people. The client has listened to them and may be stands speechless thinking of what to do.

At this point, the client has been hypnotized and has become highly suggestible, just waiting to be given an instruction. So rather than give him that instruction, they say may be, 'so you see, the choice is yours.'

Immediately, the person enters another trance and says, 'yes, I think I will think about it.' And there he goes. Notice how I made a call to action in the following excerpts from my proposals:

1.

I truly believe with all of my heart that **Definitive Guide To Home Business,** *will make a large and dramatic impact in your life. Really. See for yourself! Thank you so much for your order today and I can't wait to see what business you're creating with your* **Definitive Guide To Home Business.**

Sincerely,
Brain Reuben

2.

So here's the real question: Are you ready to take action, or are you still letting doubt stop you? Doubt is often self-sabotage at work. Are you going to control it, or let it control you?

The choice is yours. After all, if you can learn how to handle contracts for the Federal Government for only $37 and this is backed with a complete iron-clad guarantee, why in the world not do it right now?

Order today and get the exact secrets that have made those contractors you admire who they are.

Remember, when you order this material today you get unlimited access to a personal one on one consulting with me online But you must order right now.

One more thing, this is a special introductory offer to help me clear the heap of books in my garage. I end this offer without notice one the 300 books are sold off! Why take a chance on missing out?

Besides, the sooner you learn how to handle contracts for the Federal Government, the sooner you can begin living the life of your choice -- whether a new car, more money, better health, romance, happiness, or anything else you can imagine. Are you ready? Order Right Now...

To get your prospects take action is your goal. Don't assume they will figure out what to do. No, your job is to make it easy for them to say yes. In fact you don't want to give them the chance of objecting. Once you have their interest don't give them a chance if you want them to open an account with you get the forms out and even help them to start filling them, if it's a partnership you are seeking with them tell them so, if it's a job ask them to hire you. Whatever taking action means to you, just do that but never *never* end your proposals without getting your prospect to the take action   you   intend

This page is intentionally left blank

BONUS 1

FROM IDEA TO MONEY:

HOW TO GET WHATEVER YOU NEED.

...For the LORD God had not caused it to rain upon the earth, and there was not a man to till the ground. but there went up a mist from the earth, and watered the whole face of the ground. and the lord god formed man of the dust of the ground- Genesis 2:6-7

You have an idea; you want to turn into reality so that money will follow. You don't have all you require, you may need certain abilities, money, skills to work this whole thing out. How do you get it done? Yes, you will have to propose and with what you have already learnt, you can get it done. But you don't want to make the wrong effort. You want to meet someone with the capacity to help you. You can't afford to waste your effort trying to get someone invest money when the person does not have the money to invest.

First, understand that whatever ability may be required to

turn your idea to money, whether it is financial, skill or experienced is encased in some man, somewhere. You don't know this man, even though he may be your next door neighbor. He does not yet exist in your world of thought. So just like God needed a man to get His idea working, you also need a man.

How did God get the man He needed? He made him. This is what you do when you need someone in your life to get something done. You create the man!

What do you need right now to work out your idea? If it's money, how much? You don't have to cut down the amount of money you need or the skills required because whatever you need is available. Some man has that ability in the world. When you make him in your own world, your paths will cross and you will begin to see miraculous experiences in connection with the idea.

How do you get this done? Very simple.

How to Create the Man with the Ability You Need.
Your experience in life is an out picturing of your inner consciousness. There is nothing in your life that you did not

first create within you. Solomon made an emphatic statement in Proverbs 23:7 when he said, *For as he thinketh in his heart, so is he.* The Hebrew word translated thinketh is *sha'ar* which properly means to reckon. Reckon means *perceive or think about in a particular way; deem to be.* So he said that a man is an expression of his perception or estimate of himself.

Notice he did not say *as he thinketh in his heart so shall he have...* No he said, *so is he.* That means your experience is life is determined at the level of thought. So you create the man or people having the ability you require by forming the image of that man in your mind!

Once you get the image right and clear enough, you will know yourself that you have this man. Once you can possess this man in your thought, can talk to him and hear him; it will not be long before providence will cause your paths to cross. Remember, your whole world exist like thoughts in your mind. The idea is not bother yourself with the thought of how to find the man you want, but to concentrate on the reality of this man.

Consider this, Moses got an idea about the things they

needed to be built for the worship of Jehovah. But he needed people to help get his idea working. Moses did not panic because he understood this important secret. He rather focused on his idea.

Soon he got a spark of inspiration, a sudden awareness: *See, I have called by name Bezaleel the son of Uri, the son of Hur, of the tribe of Judah: And I have filled him with the spirit of God, in wisdom, and in understanding, and in knowledge, and in all manner of workmanship, To devise cunning works, to work in gold, and in silver, and in brass, And in cutting of stones, to set them, and in carving of timber, to work in all manner of workmanship. And I, behold, I have given with him Aholiab, the son of Ahisamach, of the tribe of Dan: and in the hearts of all that are wise hearted I have put wisdom, that they may make all that I have commanded thee;* Exodus 31:2-6

That's how he got it done. Its still works that way even now. To learn more ask for my book: How To Make Your Ideas Work: the secret behind ideas that rule the world. You can get it on amazon or call any of our international office lines to get it.

This page is intentionally left blank

BONUS 2

BASIC COMPONENTS OF A BUSINESS PROPOSAL.

COVER PAGE:

This is where you state your subject and your company as the case may be, the company you are writing to and the date of your presentation. Here, you either get your prospects attention or loose it forever.

EXECUTIVE SUMMARY:

This is the abstract or summary of your proposal. Here you write in simple everyday English that the lay person can understand and have a general idea of your presentation.

BODY:

That's the proposal proper. Here you lay it all down, bare and naked. You discuss fully and extensively the business you are proposing and the benefits to the prospect.

APPENDIXES:

As you deem necessary or as requested of you (as in a RFP), projects handled before, attestations, testimonials you have got come here to prove your efficiency and reliability of course

THE UNUSUAL CONCLUSION

Success in life is about knowing how the world works. When you fail to get the results you intend it is a feed back to you that you approached your target wrongly. All you require then is get to understand the situation completely and do things the right way and you will win.

Getting your ideas out to the world successfully simply requires knowing how to communicate them to the right associates. Every idea requires a company to run effectively. It's always a team work. If you are going to start a new business for example, you will need to help investors see why they should bring the money(especially when you are not providing the capital yourself), employees see why they should work together with you and the public to buy this idea. So you need the ability to effectively communicate the value of this idea to all the people involved. The success of your idea depends on this.

The ideas we have discussed in this book are for everyday

living. Applying them in your personal, family and professional life will make you a extremely successful person. People disagree and even fight because of clash of ideas. Families are wrecked apart because ideas are not effectively communicated. People stay jobless for years because they are unable to get employers hire them. Men and women remain unmarried more than necessary because they could not get their ideas of marriage across to the right persons. How important this is.

Now you have got the tools you require to live your dreams and enjoy your highest potentials. As I end this book I look forward to you becoming all you can using the ideas you have learnt from this book. I trust its being a great journey together. Now you are unbeatable and unstoppable. You got the weapons you need to be an absolute success living your dreams.

PRAYER OF SALVATION

One of the smartest decisions you could ever make is to give your heart to Jesus Christ as the Lord of your life.

It's important you understand that Jesus actually came to this world, died for the sins of the whole world and was raised again for the justification of anyone who believes in him.

The bible said in Acts 4:12, 'Neither is there salvation in any other: for there is none other name under heaven given among men, whereby we must be saved.' There is no other name but the name of Jesus Christ of Nazareth.

If you are ready to give your heart to Jesus right now, pray this prayer with me from your spirit:

Oh Lord God, I come to You, in the Name of Jesus. Your Word said that whosoever shall call on the name of Jesus shall be saved. I ask Jesus to come into my heart and be the Lord of my life. I declare He is my Lord from this day hence forth. And according to Romans 10:9-10, I declare

that I'm saved, I receive eternal life into my spirit. I'm born again. I now have Christ dwelling in me. Hallelujah.

Congratulations and welcome to God's family, Call us right now on +234 808 726 4420 or email admin@brainreuben.org so we can send you important materials that will enhance your growth and walk with the Lord.

God bless you.

ABOUT THE AUTHOR

Brian Reuben teaches attitudes and principles of an enduring successful and purposeful life.

His innovative insight into mysteries and secrets of success and his penetrating understanding of how the world works create a unique distillation of knowledge that make for excellence in life.

Brian helps companies and individuals sell, market, and communicate with precision.

He provides business leaders with innovative and thrilling ways to implement ideas to achieve tremendous personal and corporate success.

His books are on sale in all formats at leading bookstores in 165 nations. To learn more about how Brian can help you visit www.brianreubenc.org

OUR RIVETING RESOURCES

NEED A CONSULTANT FOR YOUR COMPANY OR FIRM?

Through Brian's special insight and experience he has developed business models that supersede technological, cultural and environmental limitations to work for any business, anywhere in the world. These are ideas that will help you stay above the competition level and detect the pace.

If you will write in or call today, Brian will leverage his business insight and experience in working with different types of businesses of different sizes, at different locations with divergent circumstances to create ideal business management and marketing models that will work best for your business, propelling you to unleash the full potentials of your business idea.

BRIAN REUBEN'S SEMINARS, AND WORKSHOPS help companies and individuals sell, market, and communicate more effectively. His innovative research into the mind and penetrating understanding of how the world works create a unique distillation of information never before released. Each customized program he leads is fit specifically to the needs of the organization. Brian gives his audiences innovative and thrilling ways to implement ideas to achieve tremendous success.

SPECIAL OFFER!

Apply for: **From Idea To Money**
Seminar FREE!...

From Brian Rueben

Dear Friend,

For the past 12 years, I've been helping people like you turn ALL kinds of ideas to MONEY.

I've helped people turn...

REAL ESTATE *IDEAS*
BEAUTY SHOP *IDEAS*
POLITICAL *IDEAS*
HEALTH CARE *IDEAS*
CONSULTING *IDEAS*
ICT *IDEAS*
   AND MUCH MORE!

BRIAN REUBEN the author of *'From Idea To Money'*

TO MONEY!

And I can help you do the same. The key is for you to be ready. (And it looks like you are.)

Just the fact that you've decided to read *From Idea To Money*, tells me that you are ready to TURN YOUR IDEAS TO MONEY RIGHT NOW! So congratulations for taking *THE MOST IMPORTANT ACTION.*

Success is knowing how the world works. When you receive an idea what you require is to understand how to make it work. Many have walked the path you are trying to walk and their experience can help you succeed faster and bigger. This is the first step any serious person should take.

In fact, you'll be surprised at just what you can accomplish IF you just take that first step forward — just like I did years ago.

And I want to help you do just that --- starting today! Not next month. Not next week. Not tomorrow. I mean STARTING RIGHT NOW!

Let me explain...

Since last year I've been guiding people like you in turning their ideas into money through a special program called *Idea to Money Seminar*.

The results have been incredible.

Now I'd like to offer you a free ticket for my *World-Class Idea To Money Seminar*, to help ensure that you have the highest probability of success with your ideas.

Idea To Money Seminar is a special executive training where you will seat face to face with Brian Egbulonu to give undivided attention to you and your idea(s). The training can comprise up to six person and can last for as much as six hours!

You will feel POWER surging through your entire being as Brian sets you on fire to dare the impossible, smash your road block and achieve an outstanding break through in your career.

This training is designed to empower you with the cutting-edge systems, skills, and strategies you need for creating an invincible business advantage — especially during uncertain and ever-changing economic times like we have now.

I will be able to help you get the absolute most out of *From Idea To Money*.

How do I know this?

In short, I've had countless clients achieve extraordinary results in very short periods of time.

With that said, I encourage you to "super-charge" your results scheduling your free *Idea to Money Seminar* in any of the approved cities in the *United Kingdom, United States, South Africa and Nigeria*. The training will cost you nothing except logistics, and you will leave with some powerful strategies that you can implement immediately and see results!

You'll be surprised at all that you can accomplish IF you just take that first step forward.

Clearly, *ALL* my clients are extremely grateful that they took that first step.

Will you be next? You have nothing to lose.

TURN YOUR IDEA TO MONEY TODAY!

I love you,

Brian RUEBENk

(Schedule your free consultation below)

Here are **JUST A FEW of the results people reported** (many more)...

> I did not understand what opportunities I was missing until I read Brian Egbulonu's book, "From Idea To Money". The businesses I now have with some state governments and others began when I read that book. Truly enlightening, inspiring and empowering.
>
> **David. C. Onuoha**
>
> Author, *Maximizing Your Youthful Season* and President, Empowerment Center, Uyo.

> Word cannot be enough to describe the impact of my meeting with you. Thank you for *From Idea To Money Seminar.* You've given value to my business. I remain grateful.
>
> **Godswill Erondu**
>
> President, Wisdom Coach International

To schedule your FREE training contact any of our international offices:

United States: +1 206 888 2798,
United Kingdom: +44 702 408 1389,
Nigeria: +234 808 726 4420.

www.ingramcontent.com/pod-product-compliance
Lightning Source LLC
Chambersburg PA
CBHW021431170526
45164CB00001B/197